EMMANUEL JOSEPH

The Alchemy of Longing, Nostalgia, Solitude, and the Resilience of the Human Heart

Copyright © 2025 by Emmanuel Joseph

All rights reserved. No part of this publication may be reproduced, stored or transmitted in any form or by any means, electronic, mechanical, photocopying, recording, scanning, or otherwise without written permission from the publisher. It is illegal to copy this book, post it to a website, or distribute it by any other means without permission.

First edition

This book was professionally typeset on Reedsy.
Find out more at reedsy.com

Contents

1	Chapter 1: A Journey Backward	1
2	Chapter 2: The Quiet Embrace of Solitude	3
3	Chapter 3: The Resilience of the Human Heart	5
4	Chapter 4: The Alchemy of Longing	7
5	Chapter 5: Embracing the Past	9
6	Chapter 6: The Power of Presence	11
7	Chapter 7: The Dance of Solitude and Connection	13
8	Chapter 8: The Alchemy of Loss	15
9	Chapter 9: The Strength of Vulnerability	17
10	Chapter 10: The Healing Power of Nature	19
11	Chapter 11: The Wisdom of Age	21
12	Chapter 12: The Power of Storytelling	23
13	Chapter 13: The Gift of Compassion	25
14	Chapter 14: The Quest for Meaning	27
15	Chapter 15: The Joy of Simple Pleasures	29
16	Chapter 16: The Power of Gratitude	31
17	Chapter 17: The Alchemy of Hope	33

1

Chapter 1: A Journey Backward

Nostalgia, the bittersweet essence that permeates our memories, draws us into the past with an irresistible pull. It is a force that transcends time, allowing us to relive moments long gone and reconnect with our former selves. The scent of freshly baked bread, the sound of a long-forgotten song, or the touch of a cherished object can transport us to a different era, evoking a whirlwind of emotions. Nostalgia weaves a tapestry of recollections, each thread a testament to the experiences that have shaped us.

As we traverse the landscape of our memories, we find ourselves both comforted and haunted by the past. The warmth of familial gatherings, the laughter of friends, and the innocence of childhood play are juxtaposed with the pain of lost opportunities, broken dreams, and unfulfilled promises. Nostalgia serves as a bridge between who we were and who we have become, reminding us that our past is an integral part of our present.

Yet, nostalgia is not merely a sentimental indulgence; it is a catalyst for introspection and growth. By revisiting our memories, we gain insight into our values, beliefs, and aspirations. We come to understand the choices we have made and the paths we have taken, allowing us to forge a deeper connection with ourselves. In this way, nostalgia becomes an alchemical process, transforming the raw materials of our experiences into the gold of self-awareness.

Ultimately, the journey backward is a journey inward. As we delve into the depths of our memories, we uncover the essence of our being. We come to appreciate the resilience of the human heart, which, despite the passage of time and the weight of regret, continues to beat with hope and longing. Nostalgia, then, is not a mere escape from the present but a powerful force that shapes our understanding of ourselves and our place in the world.

2

Chapter 2: The Quiet Embrace of Solitude

Solitude, often misunderstood as loneliness, is a state of being that allows us to connect with our innermost selves. It is in the quiet moments of isolation that we can truly listen to the whispers of our hearts and the echoes of our thoughts. Solitude provides a sanctuary where we can reflect on our experiences, contemplate our desires, and explore the depths of our souls.

In the embrace of solitude, we find the freedom to be ourselves without the constraints of societal expectations or the judgments of others. We can shed the masks we wear and reveal our true nature, allowing us to cultivate a sense of authenticity and self-acceptance. It is in these moments of introspection that we can gain clarity and perspective, enabling us to navigate the complexities of life with greater confidence and resilience.

The practice of solitude also fosters creativity and innovation. By removing external distractions and immersing ourselves in the quietude of our minds, we can tap into a wellspring of inspiration and ideas. This creative solitude allows us to explore new possibilities, solve problems, and envision a future that is aligned with our deepest aspirations. In this way, solitude becomes a crucible for personal and intellectual growth.

Moreover, solitude teaches us the value of presence and mindfulness. As we learn to be comfortable with our own company, we become more attuned to the subtleties of our emotions and the nuances of our thoughts. This heightened awareness enables us to engage more fully with the present moment and appreciate the beauty of the world around us. Solitude, then, is not a state of isolation but a profound opportunity for self-discovery and growth.

3

Chapter 3: The Resilience of the Human Heart

The human heart, a symbol of both vulnerability and strength, possesses an extraordinary capacity for resilience. It is in the face of adversity that we discover the true depth of our courage and the power of our spirit. The trials and tribulations we encounter serve as opportunities to test our limits, challenge our beliefs, and ultimately emerge stronger and more resilient.

Resilience is not merely the ability to endure hardship; it is the capacity to transform adversity into growth and wisdom. When we confront pain, loss, or disappointment, we have the choice to either succumb to despair or rise above our circumstances. It is through this alchemical process that we forge a stronger, more resilient self, capable of navigating the uncertainties of life with grace and determination.

The journey of resilience is also a journey of connection. As we face our challenges, we come to understand the importance of support and companionship. The bonds we form with others provide us with the strength and encouragement we need to persevere. In turn, our resilience inspires and uplifts those around us, creating a ripple effect that extends beyond our individual experiences.

Moreover, resilience is rooted in the ability to find meaning and purpose in our struggles. By reframing our challenges as opportunities for growth, we can transform our pain into a source of strength and empowerment. This shift in perspective allows us to embrace the fullness of our humanity, acknowledging both our vulnerabilities and our capacities for greatness. The resilience of the human heart, then, is a testament to the indomitable spirit that resides within each of us.

4

Chapter 4: The Alchemy of Longing

Longing, a deep and often unfulfilled desire, is a powerful force that shapes our lives and propels us forward. It is the ache for something more, the yearning for a connection or experience that transcends the ordinary. Longing is both a source of inspiration and a reminder of our humanity, revealing the depth of our passions and the intricacies of our souls.

The alchemy of longing lies in its ability to transform our desires into action. When we are driven by a profound yearning, we become motivated to pursue our dreams, seek out new experiences, and forge meaningful connections. This process of transformation is not always easy, as it requires us to confront our fears, take risks, and embrace the unknown. Yet, it is through this journey that we discover our true potential and the resilience of our spirit.

Longing also serves as a bridge between our past, present, and future. It connects us to the memories of what once was, the reality of what is, and the dreams of what could be. This continuum of longing allows us to navigate the complexities of our lives with a sense of purpose and direction. By honoring our desires and acknowledging the depth of our yearning, we can create a life that is rich with meaning and fulfillment.

Ultimately, the alchemy of longing is a testament to the resilience of the human heart. It is through our desires that we find the strength to persevere, the courage to dream, and the wisdom to grow. Longing, then, is not a weakness but a powerful force that drives us toward self-discovery and transformation. It is the alchemical process that transforms our deepest desires into the gold of a fulfilled and purposeful life.

5

Chapter 5: Embracing the Past

The past, with its myriad experiences and memories, holds a profound influence on our present and future. It is a repository of lessons learned, joys experienced, and sorrows endured. By embracing the past, we can gain a deeper understanding of ourselves and the forces that have shaped our lives. This process of reflection and acceptance is a crucial aspect of the alchemy of longing.

To embrace the past is to acknowledge its impact on our present selves. It is to recognize the significance of our experiences and the ways in which they have shaped our identities. This acknowledgment allows us to integrate the lessons of the past into our current lives, providing us with the wisdom and insight needed to navigate the challenges of the present.

Embracing the past also involves a process of healing and forgiveness. It requires us to confront the pain and regrets that may linger in our memories and to seek closure and resolution. This process of healing allows us to release the emotional burdens that weigh us down, freeing us to move forward with a sense of clarity and purpose. In this way, the past becomes a source of strength and resilience, rather than a hindrance.

Moreover, embracing the past enables us to honor the connections and relationships that have shaped our lives. It allows us to appreciate the people who have supported us, the moments that have brought us joy, and the experiences that have enriched our souls. By celebrating these connections, we can cultivate a sense of gratitude and fulfillment that enhances our present and future endeavors. The alchemy of longing, then, is rooted in the ability to embrace the past and transform it into a source of wisdom and strength.

6

Chapter 6: The Power of Presence

Presence, the state of being fully engaged in the moment, is a powerful antidote to the restless yearning of longing. It is the practice of mindfulness, the ability to savor the present and appreciate the beauty of the here and now. In a world that is constantly pulling us in different directions, the power of presence allows us to find stillness and clarity amidst the chaos.

The practice of presence involves cultivating an awareness of our thoughts, emotions, and sensations. It is the ability to observe our experiences without judgment or distraction, allowing us to engage more fully with the world around us. This heightened awareness enables us to connect with ourselves and others on a deeper level, fostering a sense of empathy and understanding.

Presence also allows us to savor the richness of life. By being fully engaged in the moment, we can appreciate the simple pleasures and joys that often go unnoticed. The warmth of the sun on our skin, the sound of laughter, the taste of a delicious meal – these are the moments that bring meaning and fulfillment to our lives. By practicing presence, we can cultivate a sense of gratitude and contentment that enhances our overall well-being.

Moreover, the power of presence enables us to navigate the challenges of life with greater resilience. By remaining grounded in the present moment, we can face adversity with a clear mind and an open heart. This mindful approach allows us to respond to difficult situations with equanimity and grace, rather than reacting impulsively out of fear or frustration. In this way, presence becomes a powerful tool for cultivating inner strength and emotional stability.

The practice of presence also fosters a deeper connection with others. When we are fully present, we can listen more attentively, empathize more deeply, and communicate more effectively. This heightened awareness allows us to build stronger, more meaningful relationships, creating a sense of community and belonging. By embracing the power of presence, we can enrich our lives and the lives of those around us.

Ultimately, the power of presence is a testament to the resilience of the human heart. It is through our ability to be fully engaged in the moment that we find the strength to persevere, the courage to dream, and the wisdom to grow. Presence, then, is not a fleeting state but a profound practice that shapes our understanding of ourselves and our place in the world.

7

Chapter 7: The Dance of Solitude and Connection

The interplay between solitude and connection is a delicate dance that shapes the human experience. While solitude provides us with the space for introspection and self-discovery, connection offers us the opportunity to share our lives with others and build meaningful relationships. The balance between these two states is essential for our overall well-being and personal growth.

Solitude allows us to retreat from the noise and demands of the external world, providing us with the time and space to reconnect with our inner selves. It is in these moments of quiet reflection that we can gain clarity and insight, allowing us to better understand our desires, values, and aspirations. This self-awareness, in turn, enables us to form more authentic and fulfilling connections with others.

Connection, on the other hand, enriches our lives by providing us with a sense of belonging and support. Through our relationships with family, friends, and community, we find the strength and encouragement needed to navigate the challenges of life. These connections also serve as a source of joy and fulfillment, reminding us of the beauty and richness of the human experience.

The dance of solitude and connection is a dynamic process that requires mindfulness and intention. It is important to recognize when we need to retreat into solitude for self-renewal and when we need to seek out connection for support and companionship. By cultivating a balance between these two states, we can create a life that is both grounded and expansive, allowing us to thrive in both our inner and outer worlds.

Ultimately, the dance of solitude and connection is a testament to the resilience of the human heart. It is through our ability to navigate the interplay between these two states that we find the strength to persevere, the courage to dream, and the wisdom to grow. Solitude and connection, then, are not opposing forces but complementary aspects of the human experience that shape our understanding of ourselves and our place in the world.

8

Chapter 8: The Alchemy of Loss

Loss, an inevitable part of the human experience, is a powerful force that shapes our lives and tests our resilience. It is through the pain of loss that we come to understand the depth of our attachments and the fragility of our existence. The alchemy of loss lies in its ability to transform our suffering into growth and wisdom, revealing the resilience of the human heart.

The experience of loss can take many forms, from the death of a loved one to the end of a relationship, the loss of a job, or the passing of a cherished dream. Each of these experiences brings with it a unique blend of emotions, including grief, anger, and despair. Yet, it is through the process of mourning and healing that we can find the strength to move forward and rebuild our lives.

The alchemy of loss involves a process of transformation that begins with acceptance. By acknowledging the reality of our loss and allowing ourselves to fully experience our emotions, we can begin the journey of healing. This process of acceptance is not about forgetting or minimizing our pain but about honoring our experience and finding meaning in our suffering.

As we navigate the journey of loss, we also discover the importance of resilience and adaptability. Loss challenges us to reevaluate our priorities, reassess our goals, and find new ways to move forward. It is through this process of adaptation that we can transform our pain into a source of strength and empowerment. The resilience of the human heart, then, is a testament to our ability to endure and grow in the face of adversity.

Moreover, the alchemy of loss teaches us the value of compassion and connection. As we confront our own pain, we develop a deeper understanding of the suffering of others, fostering a sense of empathy and solidarity. This shared experience of loss can bring us closer together, creating a sense of community and support that helps us navigate the challenges of life.

Ultimately, the alchemy of loss is a testament to the resilience of the human heart. It is through our ability to transform our suffering into growth and wisdom that we find the strength to persevere, the courage to dream, and the wisdom to grow. Loss, then, is not an end but a beginning – a powerful force that shapes our understanding of ourselves and our place in the world.

9

Chapter 9: The Strength of Vulnerability

Vulnerability, often perceived as a weakness, is a profound source of strength and resilience. It is through our willingness to embrace our vulnerabilities that we can forge deeper connections, cultivate self-awareness, and navigate the complexities of life with authenticity and courage. The strength of vulnerability lies in its ability to transform our fears and insecurities into opportunities for growth and connection.

Embracing vulnerability requires us to confront our fears and insecurities head-on. It is the willingness to acknowledge our imperfections, admit our mistakes, and share our true selves with others. This process of self-disclosure can be daunting, as it exposes us to the risk of rejection and judgment. Yet, it is through this act of vulnerability that we can cultivate a sense of authenticity and self-acceptance.

Vulnerability also plays a crucial role in building meaningful connections with others. When we are willing to share our true selves, we create a space for others to do the same. This mutual exchange of vulnerability fosters a sense of trust and intimacy, allowing us to form deeper and more fulfilling relationships. By embracing our vulnerabilities, we can break down the barriers that separate us and create a sense of community and belonging.

Moreover, the strength of vulnerability lies in its ability to foster resilience and adaptability. By confronting our fears and insecurities, we develop the courage and confidence needed to navigate the challenges of life. Vulnerability teaches us to be open to new experiences, take risks, and embrace the unknown. This willingness to step outside our comfort zones allows us to grow and evolve, ultimately strengthening our resilience.

The strength of vulnerability is also rooted in the power of self-compassion. By acknowledging our imperfections and treating ourselves with kindness and understanding, we can cultivate a sense of inner peace and resilience. This self-compassion enables us to navigate the ups and downs of life with greater equanimity and grace, allowing us to persevere in the face of adversity.

Ultimately, the strength of vulnerability is a testament to the resilience of the human heart. It is through our willingness to embrace our vulnerabilities that we find the strength to persevere, the courage to dream, and the wisdom to grow. Vulnerability, then, is not a weakness but a powerful force that shapes our understanding of ourselves and our place in the world.

10

Chapter 10: The Healing Power of Nature

Nature, with its vast beauty and tranquil presence, has the power to heal and rejuvenate the human spirit. It provides a sanctuary where we can escape the demands of daily life and reconnect with the rhythms of the natural world. The healing power of nature lies in its ability to soothe our minds, uplift our hearts, and restore our sense of balance and well-being.

Spending time in nature allows us to slow down and appreciate the simple pleasures of life. The sight of a blooming flower, the sound of birdsong, the feel of the earth beneath our feet – these sensory experiences ground us in the present moment and remind us of the interconnectedness of all living things. By immersing ourselves in nature, we can find solace and inspiration, allowing us to navigate the complexities of life with greater clarity and resilience.

Nature also serves as a powerful metaphor for the cycles of growth and renewal. Just as the seasons change and the landscape evolves, we too are constantly growing and transforming. This awareness of the natural cycles can help us embrace the ebb and flow of life, recognizing that periods of struggle and loss are often followed by moments of growth and renewal. In this way, nature becomes a source of wisdom and strength, guiding us through the challenges and transitions of life.

Moreover, the healing power of nature is rooted in its ability to foster a sense of connection and belonging. By spending time in natural environments, we can develop a deeper appreciation for the beauty and intricacies of the world around us. This sense of connection can inspire us to take better care of ourselves and the planet, fostering a sense of stewardship and responsibility. The healing power of nature, then, is not just a personal experience but a call to action to protect and preserve the natural world for future generations.

Ultimately, the healing power of nature is a testament to the resilience of the human heart. It is through our connection to the natural world that we find the strength to persevere, the courage to dream, and the wisdom to grow. Nature, then, is not just a backdrop to our lives but a vital source of healing and inspiration that shapes our understanding of ourselves and our place in the world.

11

Chapter 11: The Wisdom of Age

Age, often seen as a marker of decline, is also a wellspring of wisdom and resilience. It is through the passage of time and the accumulation of experiences that we gain insight and understanding, allowing us to navigate the complexities of life with greater clarity and grace. The wisdom of age lies in its ability to transform our struggles and triumphs into valuable lessons that shape our understanding of ourselves and the world around us.

As we grow older, we develop a deeper appreciation for the nuances and subtleties of life. We learn to see the beauty in the ordinary, to find joy in the simple pleasures, and to recognize the value of patience and perseverance. This shift in perspective allows us to approach life's challenges with a sense of calm and equanimity, knowing that we have the strength and resilience to overcome whatever obstacles come our way.

The wisdom of age also involves a process of self-discovery and acceptance. As we reflect on our past experiences, we gain a deeper understanding of our values, beliefs, and desires. This self-awareness allows us to live more authentically, embracing our true selves and letting go of the need for external validation. By cultivating a sense of inner peace and self-acceptance, we can navigate the complexities of life with greater confidence and resilience.

Moreover, the wisdom of age fosters a sense of connection and empathy. As we accumulate experiences and insights, we develop a greater understanding of the struggles and triumphs of others. This sense of empathy allows us to build stronger, more meaningful relationships, creating a sense of community and support that enhances our overall well-being. The wisdom of age, then, is not just a personal journey but a shared experience that enriches our lives and the lives of those around us.

Ultimately, the wisdom of age is a testament to the resilience of the human heart. It is through our ability to transform our experiences into valuable lessons that we find the strength to persevere, the courage to dream, and the wisdom to grow. Age, then, is not a marker of decline but a powerful source of wisdom and resilience that shapes our understanding of ourselves and our place in the world.

12

Chapter 12: The Power of Storytelling

Storytelling, an ancient and universal art form, has the power to connect, inspire, and transform. It is through the sharing of stories that we can convey our experiences, express our emotions, and communicate our values. The power of storytelling lies in its ability to bridge the gap between individuals, fostering a sense of empathy and understanding that transcends cultural and temporal boundaries.

Stories have the unique ability to engage our imagination and evoke our emotions. They transport us to different worlds, allowing us to experience the joys, sorrows, and triumphs of others. This immersive experience fosters a sense of empathy, enabling us to see the world through the eyes of others and understand their perspectives. By engaging with stories, we can develop a deeper appreciation for the diversity of human experiences and the common threads that unite us all.

Storytelling also serves as a powerful tool for personal and collective growth. By sharing our stories, we can process our experiences, make sense of our emotions, and gain insight into our lives. This process of reflection and expression allows us to cultivate self-awareness and resilience, enabling us to navigate the complexities of life with greater clarity and confidence. Moreover, the act of storytelling fosters a sense of connection and community, creating a space where we can support and uplift one another.

The power of storytelling extends beyond personal experiences, shaping our understanding of history, culture, and identity. Through the stories of our ancestors, we can gain insight into the challenges and triumphs of the past, allowing us to appreciate the richness of our heritage and the resilience of the human spirit. These collective stories provide us with a sense of belonging and continuity, grounding us in the present while guiding us toward the future.

Ultimately, the power of storytelling is a testament to the resilience of the human heart. It is through our ability to share our experiences and connect with others that we find the strength to persevere, the courage to dream, and the wisdom to grow. Storytelling, then, is not just an art form but a powerful force that shapes our understanding of ourselves and our place in the world.

13

Chapter 13: The Gift of Compassion

Compassion, the ability to empathize with the suffering of others and respond with kindness and understanding, is a powerful force that shapes our lives and our relationships. It is through the practice of compassion that we can cultivate a sense of connection, foster a sense of community, and navigate the complexities of life with grace and resilience. The gift of compassion lies in its ability to transform our hearts and minds, allowing us to become more attuned to the needs of others and more responsive to the challenges of the world.

The practice of compassion begins with the cultivation of empathy. By putting ourselves in the shoes of others and seeking to understand their experiences and emotions, we can develop a deeper sense of connection and solidarity. This empathetic awareness allows us to see the world through the eyes of others, fostering a sense of understanding and appreciation for the diversity of human experiences.

Compassion also involves a willingness to take action in response to the suffering of others. It is not enough to simply feel empathy; we must also be willing to extend a helping hand and offer our support. This active practice of compassion can take many forms, from small acts of kindness to larger efforts to address social and systemic injustices. By responding to the needs of others with kindness and generosity, we can create a ripple effect of positive change that extends beyond our individual actions.

The gift of compassion also fosters a sense of resilience and well-being. By focusing on the needs of others and seeking to alleviate their suffering, we can cultivate a sense of purpose and fulfillment that enhances our overall well-being. This sense of purpose allows us to navigate the challenges of life with greater clarity and confidence, knowing that our actions are making a positive difference in the world.

Moreover, the practice of compassion strengthens our relationships and creates a sense of community. By extending kindness and understanding to others, we build trust and foster a sense of belonging. This sense of community provides us with the support and encouragement we need to persevere in the face of adversity, creating a network of resilience that enhances our overall well-being.

Ultimately, the gift of compassion is a testament to the resilience of the human heart. It is through our ability to empathize with the suffering of others and respond with kindness and understanding that we find the strength to persevere, the courage to dream, and the wisdom to grow. Compassion, then, is not just a virtue but a powerful force that shapes our understanding of ourselves and our place in the world.

14

Chapter 14: The Quest for Meaning

The quest for meaning is a fundamental aspect of the human experience, driving us to seek out purpose and understanding in our lives. It is through this quest that we can navigate the complexities of life, find fulfillment in our experiences, and cultivate a sense of resilience and well-being. The quest for meaning lies in its ability to transform our struggles and triumphs into a coherent narrative that shapes our understanding of ourselves and our place in the world.

The search for meaning often begins with a process of introspection and reflection. By examining our experiences, values, and beliefs, we can gain insight into what truly matters to us and what gives our lives purpose. This self-awareness allows us to make intentional choices that align with our deepest aspirations, creating a sense of direction and fulfillment in our lives.

The quest for meaning also involves a willingness to embrace uncertainty and ambiguity. Life is filled with moments of uncertainty and change, and it is through our ability to navigate these moments that we can find meaning and purpose. By embracing the unknown and remaining open to new experiences, we can cultivate a sense of curiosity and wonder that enriches our lives. This openness allows us to explore new possibilities, discover hidden talents, and find meaning in unexpected places. It is through this process of exploration and discovery that we can create a life that is rich with purpose and fulfillment.

The quest for meaning also involves a commitment to personal growth and development. By continually seeking to learn, grow, and evolve, we can unlock our full potential and create a life that is aligned with our deepest aspirations. This commitment to growth requires us to embrace challenges, take risks, and persevere in the face of adversity. In this way, the quest for meaning becomes a journey of resilience and transformation.

Moreover, the quest for meaning is deeply connected to our relationships and connections with others. By building meaningful relationships and contributing to the well-being of our communities, we can find a sense of purpose and fulfillment that extends beyond our individual experiences. This sense of connection and contribution allows us to create a legacy that enriches the lives of others and shapes the world for the better.

Ultimately, the quest for meaning is a testament to the resilience of the human heart. It is through our ability to seek out purpose and understanding that we find the strength to persevere, the courage to dream, and the wisdom to grow. Meaning, then, is not a destination but a continuous journey that shapes our understanding of ourselves and our place in the world.

15

Chapter 15: The Joy of Simple Pleasures

In the hustle and bustle of modern life, it is easy to overlook the simple pleasures that bring joy and fulfillment to our lives. These moments of everyday beauty and delight are often the most meaningful and memorable, providing us with a sense of contentment and well-being. The joy of simple pleasures lies in their ability to ground us in the present moment and remind us of the richness of life.

Simple pleasures can take many forms, from a quiet cup of tea in the morning to a walk in the park, from the laughter of children to the warmth of a hug. These moments of joy are not dependent on external achievements or material possessions but are rooted in our ability to appreciate the beauty and wonder of the world around us. By cultivating an awareness of these simple pleasures, we can enhance our overall well-being and create a life that is rich with meaning and fulfillment.

The practice of mindfulness is a powerful tool for experiencing the joy of simple pleasures. By paying attention to our thoughts, emotions, and sensations, we can fully engage with the present moment and savor the richness of our experiences. This mindful awareness allows us to appreciate the small moments of joy that often go unnoticed, creating a sense of gratitude and contentment that enhances our overall well-being.

Moreover, the joy of simple pleasures is deeply connected to our relationships and connections with others. By sharing these moments of joy with loved ones, we can strengthen our bonds and create lasting memories that enrich our lives. This sense of connection and belonging provides us with the support and encouragement we need to navigate the challenges of life, fostering a sense of resilience and well-being.

Ultimately, the joy of simple pleasures is a testament to the resilience of the human heart. It is through our ability to find joy in the everyday moments of life that we find the strength to persevere, the courage to dream, and the wisdom to grow. Simple pleasures, then, are not just fleeting moments of happiness but powerful sources of meaning and fulfillment that shape our understanding of ourselves and our place in the world.

16

Chapter 16: The Power of Gratitude

Gratitude, the practice of acknowledging and appreciating the positive aspects of our lives, is a powerful force that shapes our well-being and resilience. It is through the practice of gratitude that we can cultivate a sense of contentment, foster a sense of connection, and navigate the complexities of life with grace and resilience. The power of gratitude lies in its ability to transform our perspective and enhance our overall well-being.

The practice of gratitude begins with a shift in mindset. By focusing on the positive aspects of our lives and acknowledging the blessings we have received, we can cultivate a sense of abundance and contentment. This shift in perspective allows us to appreciate the beauty and richness of our experiences, creating a sense of fulfillment and well-being that enhances our overall quality of life.

Gratitude also fosters a sense of connection and empathy. By acknowledging the contributions and support of others, we can strengthen our relationships and create a sense of community and belonging. This sense of connection provides us with the support and encouragement we need to navigate the challenges of life, fostering a sense of resilience and well-being.

Moreover, the practice of gratitude enhances our overall well-being by promoting positive emotions and reducing stress. By focusing on the positive aspects of our lives, we can cultivate a sense of joy and contentment that counteracts the negative effects of stress and anxiety. This positive emotional state allows us to navigate the ups and downs of life with greater equanimity and grace, fostering a sense of resilience and well-being.

Ultimately, the power of gratitude is a testament to the resilience of the human heart. It is through our ability to acknowledge and appreciate the positive aspects of our lives that we find the strength to persevere, the courage to dream, and the wisdom to grow. Gratitude, then, is not just a fleeting emotion but a powerful practice that shapes our understanding of ourselves and our place in the world.

17

Chapter 17: The Alchemy of Hope

Hope, the belief in the possibility of a better future, is a powerful force that shapes our lives and propels us forward. It is through the practice of hope that we can navigate the challenges of life, find meaning in our experiences, and cultivate a sense of resilience and well-being. The alchemy of hope lies in its ability to transform our struggles and triumphs into a coherent narrative that shapes our understanding of ourselves and our place in the world.

The practice of hope begins with a vision of a better future. By imagining the possibilities and envisioning a brighter tomorrow, we can cultivate a sense of optimism and motivation that propels us forward. This vision of the future allows us to set goals, make plans, and take action, creating a sense of purpose and direction that enhances our overall well-being.

Hope also involves a willingness to persevere in the face of adversity. Life is filled with moments of struggle and uncertainty, and it is through our ability to maintain hope that we can navigate these challenges with resilience and determination. By focusing on the possibilities and believing in our ability to overcome obstacles, we can cultivate a sense of strength and empowerment that enables us to persevere in the face of adversity.

Moreover, the alchemy of hope is deeply connected to our relationships and connections with others. By sharing our hopes and dreams with loved ones, we can create a sense of community and support that enhances our overall well-being. This sense of connection provides us with the encouragement and motivation we need to pursue our dreams and navigate the challenges of life.

Ultimately, the alchemy of hope is a testament to the resilience of the human heart. It is through our ability to believe in the possibility of a better future that we find the strength to persevere, the courage to dream, and the wisdom to grow. Hope, then, is not just a fleeting emotion but a powerful practice that shapes our understanding of ourselves and our place in the world.

Book Description

"**The Alchemy of Longing: Nostalgia, Solitude, and the Resilience of the Human Heart**" is a profound exploration of the human experience, delving into the intricate interplay between longing, solitude, and resilience. Through seventeen eloquent chapters, the book examines the transformative power of nostalgia, the quiet embrace of solitude, and the extraordinary capacity of the human heart to persevere and grow.

Each chapter weaves together thoughtful reflections and compelling narratives, offering readers a rich tapestry of insights and wisdom. From the journey backward into our memories to the alchemy of longing, the power of presence, the dance of solitude and connection, and the resilience found in vulnerability, this book provides a deep and nuanced understanding of the human condition.

"The Alchemy of Longing" invites readers to embrace the beauty of the past, find solace in the present, and cultivate hope for the future. It is a testament to the resilience of the human spirit and a celebration of the interconnectedness of our experiences. Through its pages, readers will discover the strength to navigate life's challenges, the courage to pursue their dreams, and the wisdom to grow and transform.

This book is a heartfelt tribute to the enduring power of longing, solitude, and resilience, offering readers a timeless guide to understanding themselves and their place in the world.

www.ingramcontent.com/pod-product-compliance
Lightning Source LLC
LaVergne TN
LVHW010441070526
838199LV00066B/6128